CORETTA SCOTT KING

DISCOVER THE LIFE OF AN AMERICAN LEGEND

David and Patricia Armentrout

Rourke

Publishing LLC
Vero Beach, Florida 32964

www.rourkepublishing.com

PHOTO CREDITS: © Getty Images, Cover; © Hulton/Archive by Getty Images, page 18; © Library of Congress all other photos

Cover: *Coretta Scott King*
Title page : *Coretta Scott King and Martin Luther King, Jr. meet New York City mayor Robert Wagner.*

Editor: Frank Sloan

Cover design by Nicola Stratford

Library of Congress Cataloging-in-Publication Data

Armentrout, David, 1962-
  Coretta Scott King / David and Patricia Armentrout.
    v. cm. — (Discover the life of an American legend)
Includes bibliographical references and index.
Contents: Coretta Scott King — Early life — Coretta meets Martin — Rosa
Parks — The bus boycott — Living in Alabama — Martin is assassinated — The King Center — Coretta's
hard work — Dates to remember.
  ISBN 1-58952-659-7 (hardcover)
  1. King, Coretta Scott, 1927—Juvenile literature. 2. African American women civil rights workers—
Biography—Juvenile literature. 3. Civil rights workers—United States—Biography—Juvenile literature. 4.
African Americans—Biography—Juvenile literature. 5. King, Martin Luther, Jr., 1929-1968—Juvenile
literature. 6. African Americans—Civil rights—United States—History—20th century—Juvenile literature. 7.
Civil rights movements—United States—History—20th century—Juvenile literature. [1. King, Coretta Scott,
1927- 2. Civil rights workers. 3. Women—Biography. 4. African Americans—Biography.]
  I. Armentrout, Patricia, 1960- II. Title. III. Series.
  E185.97.K47A76 2003
  323'.092--dc21   2003002205

Printed in the USA

CG/CG

Table of Contents

Coretta Scott King

Coretta Scott King is the **widow** of the Reverend Dr. Martin Luther King, Jr. Coretta and Martin formed one of the greatest **nonviolent civil rights** movements in America. Coretta Scott King and her children continue to fight for peace, justice, and equality worldwide.

The goal of the civil rights movement was equal treatment for all races.

Early Life

Coretta Scott was born in Alabama in 1927. She grew up during the Great Depression. It was a time when thousands of workers lost their jobs. Many people barely had enough money to survive. It was also a time of **segregation** in the South. Whites and blacks were kept apart in places such as restaurants, movie theaters, and schools.

Black Americans were forced to use separate entrances to movie theaters.

Coretta Meets Martin

Coretta left Alabama in 1945 to attend college in Ohio. Her favorite subject was music. Coretta studied music in Boston, too. There she met Martin Luther King, Jr. They shared many goals. They both wanted to help African Americans get good jobs and achieve civil rights. Coretta and Martin married in 1953. Later they had four children.

Coretta Scott and Martin Luther King, Jr. married in 1953.

Rosa Parks

The Kings moved to Montgomery, Alabama in 1954. The Montgomery Bus Company had unfair rules for black passengers. Blacks had to sit in the back and give up their seats to white passengers if the front seats were full. One day a black woman named Rosa Parks refused to give up her seat to a white passenger. She was arrested and taken to jail.

Rosa Parks' protest led to a boycott of the Montgomery Bus Company.

The Bus Boycott

After Rosa Parks was arrested, Martin suggested a bus **boycott**—a refusal to ride the bus in protest against the unfair rules. The boycott lasted a year. In 1956, the Supreme Court put a stop to the unfair rules of the Montgomery Bus Company. That year was very hard on the King family. Some people, who were against civil rights for African Americans, threatened the Kings with violence.

Martin Luther King, Jr. fought for equal rights for all Americans.

13

Living in Atlanta

The Kings moved to Atlanta and continued to organize nonviolent protests against **racism**. Martin spoke at many events across the country. Coretta sang at "Freedom Concerts." Coretta cared for their four children and also traveled and spoke out for world peace.

The King family was followed closely by reporters.

Martin Is Assassinated

Many people were angry about Martin's fight for civil rights. He was attacked and sometimes arrested for his peaceful protests. Coretta feared for her husband's safety.

On April 4, 1968, Martin Luther King, Jr. was **assassinated.** Coretta showed everyone how strong she was. The day before Martin's funeral, Coretta marched for civil rights in his place.

Coretta traveled throughout the world speaking and performing at public gatherings.

The King Center

Coretta founded the Martin Luther King, Jr., Center for Nonviolent Social Change. It is part of the Martin Luther King, Jr. National Historic Site in Atlanta. The center is a living memorial to Martin Luther King, Jr. It includes Martin's birth home, a library, many exhibits, and Dr. King's tomb.

Coretta became a recognized civil rights leader and public speaker.

Coretta's Hard Work

The first Coretta Scott King Award was given in 1970. The award honors Coretta's courage and strength. It is presented to black authors and illustrators.

Dr. and Mrs. King are admired for leading the greatest nonviolent civil rights movement in America.

Coretta worked for years to make Martin's birthday a national holiday. Congress approved the plan in 1986. The third Monday in January is Martin Luther King Day. It is the first American holiday dedicated to an African American.

Dates to Remember

1927	Born April 27 in Alabama
1945	Attends Antioch College in Ohio
1951	Attends the New England Conservatory of Music in Boston
1952	Meets Martin Luther King, Jr.
1953	Coretta and Martin marry
1955	Rosa Parks is arrested; Coretta and Martin encourage the bus boycott
1968	Martin Luther King, Jr. is assassinated
1981	The Martin Luther King, Jr., Center for Nonviolent Social Change opens
1986	Martin Luther King Day is established

Glossary

assassinated (uh SASS uh NAYT ed) — a word that describes an important or well-known person who has been murdered

boycott (BOI kot) — to refuse to buy something or take part in something as a way of protest

civil rights (SIV il RYTZ) — rights guaranteed to all citizens to have equal treatment under the law

nonviolent (NON vigh uh lent) — not being violent; peaceful

racism (RAY sis um) — the belief that one race is superior, or better, than another

segregation (seg ruh GAY shun) — keeping people or groups apart

widow (WID oh) — the wife of a man who is dead

Index

Further Reading

King, Coretta Scott. *My Life with Martin Luther King, Jr.* Henry Holt, 1994

Klingel, Cynthia. *Coretta Scott King*. The Child's World, 1999

Websites To Visit

www.thekingcenter.com
www.galegroup.com/free_resources/whm/bio/king_c_s.htm

About The Authors

David and Patricia Armentrout have written many nonfiction books for young readers. They specialize in science and social studies topics. They have had several books published for primary school reading. The Armentrouts live in Cincinnati, Ohio, with their two children.